mapping
SOUTH AMERICA

Gareth Stevens
Publishing

By Mark Harasymiw

Please visit our website, www.garethstevens.com. For a free color catalog of all our high-quality books, call toll free 1-800-542-2595 or fax 1-877-542-2596.

Library of Congress Cataloging-in-Publication Data

Harasymiw, Mark.
Mapping South America / by Mark Harasymiw.
  p. cm. — (Mapping the World)
Includes index.
ISBN 978-1-4339-9120-2 (pbk.)
ISBN 978-1-4339-9121-9 (6-pack)
ISBN 978-1-4339-9119-6 (library binding)
1. South America—Juvenile literature. 2. South America—Geography—Juvenile literature. I. Harasymiw, Mark. II. Title.
F2208.5 H37 2014
980—d23

First Edition

Published in 2014 by
Gareth Stevens Publishing
111 East 14th Street, Suite 349
New York, NY 10003

Designer: Katelyn E. Reynolds
Editor: Kristen Rajczak

Photo credits: Cover, p. 1 (photo) Leagam/Shutterstock.com; cover, pp. 1, 15 (inset) Uwe Dedering/Wikipedia.com; cover, pp. 1–24 (banner) kanate/Shutterstock.com; cover, pp. 1–24 (series elements and cork background) iStockphoto/Thinkstock.com; p. 5 The World Factbook/CIA; p. 7 (inset) Sunshine Pics/Shutterstock.com; p. 7 (main) Elena Elisseeva/Shutterstock.com; p. 9 AridOcean/Shutterstock.com; p. 11 (inset) kastianz/Shutterstock.com; p. 11 (main) NASA/JPL/NIMA; p. 13 (inset) Dr. Morley Read/Shutterstock.com; pp. 13 (main), 17 (main), 21 (all insets) iStockphoto/Thinkstock.com; p. 15 (main) James P. Blair/National Geographic/Getty Images; p. 17 (inset) LennyWikidata/Wikipedia.com; p. 19 (inset) Eddo/Wikipedia.com; p. 19 (main) Peter Adams/Photolibrary/Getty Images; p. 20 (stamp) astudio/Shutterstock.com; p. 21 (main) dalmingo/Shutterstock.com.

Printed in the United States of America

CPSIA compliance information: Batch #CS13GS: For further information contact Gareth Stevens, New York, New York at 1-800-542-2595.

CONTENTS

Words in the glossary appear in **bold** type the first time they are used in the text.

ALL OVER THE CONTINENT

South America is a **continent** of huge rainforests, tall mountains, dry deserts, and wide grasslands. It's the fourth-largest continent by area and the fifth-largest in population. South America has the longest mountain range in the world, the largest rainforest, and the tallest waterfall.

Twelve countries make up most of South America's land area: Argentina, Bolivia, Brazil, Chile, Colombia, Ecuador, Guyana, Paraguay, Peru, Suriname, Uruguay, and Venezuela. South America makes up about one-eighth of Earth's land surface.

Where in the World?

Although considered part of the continent of South America, the Falkland Islands are owned by the United Kingdom, and French Guiana is a part of France.

Political maps like this one show countries' borders. You can see that Brazil shares a border with 10 other countries!

Scale 1:35,000,000
Azimuthal Equal-Area Projection

0   500 Kilometers
0   500 Miles

5

LOCATION, LOCATION, LOCATION

South America is located in the Western **Hemisphere**. The **equator** passes through the northern part of the continent, including the countries of Brazil, Colombia, and Ecuador.

South America is almost totally surrounded by water. The Atlantic Ocean lies to the east, the Caribbean Sea to the north and northwest, and the Pacific Ocean to the west. South America is connected to Central and North America by the **Isthmus** of Panama. At its narrowest, the isthmus is only 50 miles (80 km) wide.

Where in the World?

The southern tip of South America, Cape Horn, is only about 600 miles (965 km) from Antarctica!

6

The Mitad del Mundo is a monument that sits on the equator in Ecuador. Mitad del Mundo means "middle of the world."

equator

Mitad del Mundo

AREAS OF SOUTH AMERICA

There are three main areas of South America. On the west side of the continent are the Andes Mountains. Made up of snowy **peaks** and grassy **plateaus** that stretch along the western side of the continent, the Andes Mountains are the longest mountain range in the world.

The middle part of the continent is made up of wide plains and rainforests, and is drained by large rivers. Finally, grassy, hilly, and forested highlands are located on the eastern part of the continent.

Where in the World?

Patagonia is a region in both Chile and Argentina, in the southernmost part of South America. The Spanish explorer Ferdinand Magellan named it after the Spanish word for the local Indians, *Patagones*.

A relief map of South America shows the geographical differences around the continent.

central plains

Andes Mountains

eastern highlands

Patagonia

THE ANDES

The Andes Mountains stretch more than 5,000 miles (8,045 km) from Colombia in the north to Chile and Argentina in the south. They have the highest peaks in the Western Hemisphere, some reaching above 20,000 feet (6,096 m)! **Volcanoes** are common all along the Andes. In fact, volcanoes formed many of the high peaks of the mountains.

The Andes are also very rich in **natural resources**, such as coal and oil, and **deposits** of valuable metals, such as copper, silver, and gold.

Where in the World?

Some parts of the Andes split into two or three parallel mountain ranges called cordilleras (kohr-dee-YEHR-uhz).

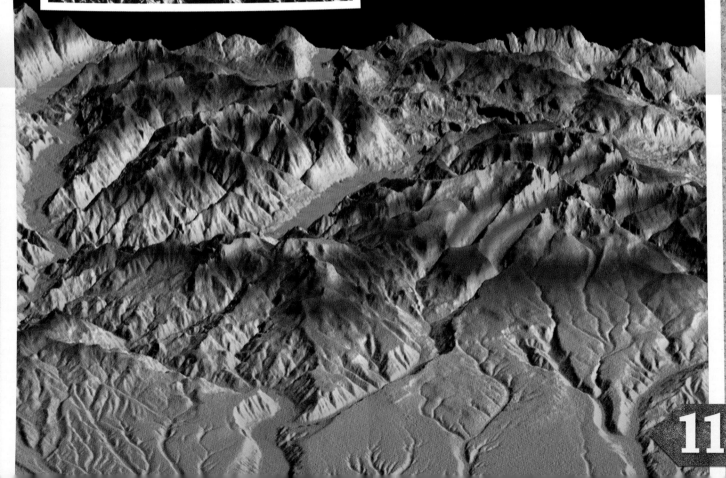

Elevation is how far above sea level something is. The map below shows the elevation of part of the Andes Mountain range. Use the map key to find the highest points!

Elevation of Laguna Mellquina, Andes Mountains, Argentina

2,300 feet   8,000 feet

CENTRAL PLAINS: THE AMAZON

The Amazon River is the second-longest river in the world, stretching about 4,000 miles (6,435 km) from the Peruvian Andes to the Atlantic Ocean. The Amazon **basin** is the name of the area around the river. Much of the basin is covered by rainforests and wetlands.

The rainforest is filled with many types of trees, a natural resource sold to other countries. In some cases, the land where trees have been cut down is used for farms that raise both crops and livestock.

Where in the World?

The Amazon rainforest is the largest rainforest in the world and makes up half of the rainforest area on Earth.

The Amazon rainforest faces many problems today as people and industries move to the area and cut down trees.

13

CENTRAL PLAINS:
LLANOS AND THE PAMPAS

To the north and the south of the Amazon basin are lowland areas. North of the Amazon are the Llanos in Colombia and Venezuela. Llanos means "plains" in Spanish. The Orinoco River bounds this area of wide grassy plains to the east, and the Andes are to the west. The Llanos are ideal for raising cattle.

South of the Amazon are the Pampas, a flat grassland in Argentina and Uruguay. The soil there is good for growing crops such as alfalfa and grapes.

Where in the World?

Before the Pampas were settled and used as farmland, cowboys, or gauchos (GOW-chohz), looked after huge herds of cattle there.

This map shows where the Llanos and Pampas are found in South America. The picture below shows an area of the Pampas in Argentina.

Llanos

Pampas

THE EASTERN HIGHLANDS AND AFRICA

If you look at a map of the world, you may notice that the east coast of South America looks as if it could fit into the western part of Africa. Many scientists believe the two were once joined and drifted apart millions of years ago. This is because of the natural movement of Earth's **plates**.

The eastern highlands of South America would have bordered Africa about 140 million years ago. Today, the Guiana Highlands cover the northeastern part of the continent, and the Brazilian Highlands cover eastern and southern Brazil.

16

Where in the World?

Eastern Brazil contains very rich deposits of gold and diamonds.

When South America and Africa were connected, they were part of a landmass scientists call Gondwana. The picture below shows the Cliffs of Mount Roraima, one of the highest points in the eastern highlands.

LAURASIA

equator

Africa

South America

GONDWANA

PEOPLE AND CULTURE

People of many different backgrounds make up South America's population. Most come from three main groups: native South Americans, Africans, and Europeans. Most Europeans are Spanish or Portuguese. Today, those living in South America are often a mix of these backgrounds.

Spanish is the official language of most countries, though some countries have other official languages. Brazil's official language is Portuguese, Guyana's is English, and Suriname's is Dutch. Unsurprisingly, in French Guiana, French is the official language.

18

Where in the World?

Two of the most populous cities in South America are Buenos Aires, Argentina, and São Paulo, Brazil.

The Languages of South America

- Spanish
- Portuguese
- English
- French
- Dutch

Besides the European languages spoken in South America, native languages are spoken in many countries as well. These languages often mix with the main languages in cities such as Salvador, Brazil, shown here, because so many people live there.

AMAZING FACTS
ABOUT SOUTH AMERICA

The world's highest waterfall is found in the Venezuelan part of the Guiana Highlands. Water drops 3,212 feet (979 m) over Angel Falls.

Lake Titicaca is the world's highest large lake. It's located between Peru and Bolivia at an elevation of 12,500 feet (3,810 m).

Aconcagua, in the Andes, is the tallest mountain in the Western Hemisphere! Aconcagua is 22,831 feet (6,959 m) tall.

ANDES
ACONCAGUA
22,831 ft.
Argentina

Where in the World?

The Atacama Desert is located in northern Chile. In some places, no rainfall has ever been recorded!

Visiting South America

Angel Falls

Lake Titicaca

Atacama Desert

Aconcagua

GLOSSARY

basin: the entire area of land drained by a river

continent: one of Earth's seven great landmasses. They are Asia, Africa, North America, South America, Antarctica, Europe, and Australia.

deposit: an amount of a mineral in the ground that builds up over a period of time

equator: an imaginary line around Earth that is the same distance from the North and the South Poles

hemisphere: one half of Earth

isthmus: a narrow strip of land connecting two larger land areas

natural resource: things in nature that can be used by people

peak: the pointed top of a mountain

plate: one of the large pieces of rock that make up Earth's outer layer

plateau: an area of level ground that is higher than the ground around it

volcano: an opening in a planet's surface through which hot, liquid rock sometimes flows

FOR MORE INFORMATION

Books

DePietro, Frank. *South American Immigrants*. Philadelphia, PA: Mason Crest Publishers, 2013.

Gibson, Karen Bush. *Spotlight on South America*. Mankato, MN: Capstone Press, 2011.

Hirsch, Rebecca E. *South America*. New York, NY: Children's Press, 2013.

Websites

Geography of South America
geography.howstuffworks.com/south-america/geography-of-south-america.htm
Read more information about the diverse continent of South America.

South America
travel.nationalgeographic.com/travel/continents/south-america/
Read facts and review maps about South American countries.

INDEX